Ravenous Bliss: new & selected love poems

10 June 2017

For Barb Hathaway,
with high regard, and
heartfelt hugs.

Jim B.

Ravenous Bliss

new & selected love poems

James Bertolino (signature)

James Bertolino

MoonPath Press

Poetry
ISBN 978-1-936657-13-1

Cover art: Anita K. Boyle
Author photo: Anita K. Boyle

Book design by Tonya Namura
using Minion Pro

MoonPath Press is dedicated to publishing the
best poets of the U.S. Northwest Pacific states

MoonPath Press
PO Box 1808
Kingston, WA 98346

MoonPathPress@yahoo.com

http://MoonPathPress.com

For Anita

Who loves, raves.
—Lord Byron

A Droplet

Royal,
> dark,
>> light-generous
and proud.

An angel
> of the first morning
joins him now,
>> holds him

as a droplet
> of dew holds

the moon.

CONTENTS

 SELECTED

1969

Abandoned

The loneliness
of the night-watchman
wandering heaven's corridors—
knowing there'll be no pay,
no mouths
to feed.

The irony
of the poet
who feels his silence
is misunderstood.

Look love,
Death walks slowly
with an empty satchel.
Our brittle bliss
has no value
for him.

The Red Dress

The whirr
of the sewing machine

her back
       bent
beautiful in the tension
of her toil

the purr
of my thread
       between
her fingers

brings her to me,
brings us,
weaves me in the house
of her

& nowhere
is there stronger
more soft
       fabric
than this.

Under Mayan Sun

Yellow
crushed meat of
raw fruit
forms islands
in blood
       lady bugs
swim
on flat stone.

The ritual dances
have ceased.

    I cross
hand
over hand
my single nerve stretched taut
to where your
virgin gold
       breasts
heave no more.

Spring.

This rite of maize
your blood
will grow tall
       & thoughtless
as blades.

My love
for you
was a fall of bones.

Yellow Spring

Everything outside
is yellow. A crater
in the sidewalk
left by the come
and go of winter, daily
fills up with
popsicle sticks.
When she passes,
the air this side my window
crackles, everything, the empty
bread-box has a red edge.
This color is me.
She smiles into the sun
above the house.
She is innocent.
I want fiercely to touch her.

1970

Divide Again

My wife yearns
to know and have
in unknown and wet streets
the sun

She would strum
few chords, but listen
attentively

Zeus, divide
again
my parts and render me
city

The warmth will come
of itself.

I Sold a Poem

You turn from me.

It's just
a normal night, we did
run out of ice,
& just perhaps
it was the trash I meant
but then forgot
to dump. I kissed your nose
the way I always do.
I agreed I should
have come home sooner. You know
I sold a poem;
you said you understood.
I would have
called
but my mouth was cold with beer.

It's no big thing.

I'm near you now & you concede
that certain times
in certain ways
I must be free.

You understand.
I understand.
                      But god,

tonight you turn from me.

I Take Thee

woman
where ruby-eyed fish
fire
the waters of night

Where delicate indigo birds
roost
till dawn

then trellis
the amber flesh of morning

over yearlings
brash
for cool mountain air

& the wordless heights
of blood

Maternal Equinox

Just as an apple
wrinkles to brown

softens with more than
the reddening
number of suns

so you my pear
will blossom to yellow
when this winter of trees

falls from
our breath
and your limbs become

a bowl of fresh fruit
waiting to be.

14

Origami Prayer

The whisper
of the delicate paper
folds her fingers

springs her East
to a bird

the wings of which
trip bright
gardens
in my heart.

When I Hold

to your shoulders
with heavy fingers

& down an eyelash roll a tear
to break on your brow

it doesn't matter
that sorcerers dance on their drums
when you pass

& neighbors call you *witch*.

1972

Egret

I think of you and
feel my fingers float off, palms
descend, egret's wings
in slow
motion toward your face, your forehead

and in
to cradle
the glowing lobes of your brain

The Marriage

I am a turtle
with a lead shell,
with fragile blue wings
of gossamer
& small.
The sky is far
when you say you're through.

You are a bobcat
with thin claws of glass,
with gray dreamy eyes
of no luster.
The green tall trees
are emery
when I say I don't love you.

Night comes.
The air is sparse,
the ground cold.
Our eyes round owls
afraid in the dark.
Give me your hand,
it will hold us.

Room

The bowl-shaped
wicker chair,
the fine contour
of narrow-necked vase,

the smoldering edges
of red,
red dahlias
pucker the air.

And you, blue
veins (your
delicate)
charge your nipples.

Your thoughts reach
hold
like a bowl
my space.

Spring Below Moscow Mtn.

The cracks
firm
lucid lines
conceived by the lake
on the frozen
skin

sweet varied song
of its year
below the mountain

now
melts away

Water's love
for rock

proclaimed

Teaching the Sun

Outside the March wind
means business.
From a winter sky
grown old & gray
the snowflakes, white stragglers,
work into dark crevices
& caves
of wet bark.

The trees, trembling,
shake black fists,
remembering with rage
their kidnapped leaves.

But wait.
A swirl, a dance of red
setting fire to the lilac bushes
near the field. It's

a girl! Lovely.
A whirl of laughter
teasing the sun from its mask
of dull clouds,

teaching the sun
to sing!

1973

Her Kiss

My head throbs
mute stunned rock
whose memory
finally comes.

Morning

With your kiss awake
on my lips
I am born

and the sheets
are incense
and flannel

and the sun
is the music
of a winter wren

and a golden animal
runs off
                    with my heart.

Skin

O god the skin
the skin
the skin

where the skin
comes together
in folds

where this togetherness
folds
folds me
in

1975

The Cold Room

Because we kept no belief

Because hunger

You reach to close my rough fingers over
a knocking at the heart

The oak table
blasphemes
the name we called love

& the walls collect
like stricken
petals
our failing breath

Light

A young woman is lying naked
on the sand.
Her clear eyes beckon
the sky.
Like a gem revolved slowly in the sun
her thoughts make love
to light.
Pleasure hovers over the beach
like prayer.

Of Sunlight

Heavy scent of spring grass
passing below

Sun

& she behind me warm
to my back
our buttocks bare to the horse's flesh

No cities
no dream
we are this naked beast
making space for our living in these hills

We move
unto each other
& are the syllables of sunlight

singing

On a Line by Charles Simic

This table is a cup
he lifts,
a receptacle of
weights & measures /
proportions

Without it he cannot
know
his own hands from
the ink a printer mixes
with water

the right proportions
or lines
will grey-out
in the poem

           He knows
the yellow cake
he likes
the chocolate frosting rich
with butter
    his mouth knows
    more
than tablespoons
of shortening, & flour /
cups of it
      spacing
his wife's
day
    Till with his hand he cups

her chin, lifts
to mix
her mouth with his

This woman is the table
of his life

On a Line by John Ashbery

The space was
magnificent and dry.
You slid your

cold hands up
beneath my sweater
whispering "I love

your body" to my ear
that I not be surprised
by the chill. Your chin

resting on my shoulder.
Together we watched
a lone gull bring down

the sun. An abrupt
shrill cry. Somewhere
off along the beach

the small life
of a bird or chipmunk
was complete.

Oregon

A rainbow
sifts
about our heads
on this butte,
the stone
ecstatic
with lichens

Birds buffet in flight
with our eyelids

A lone sheep
an odor
over the rocks
pulls roots from our blood
with its teeth

& ruminating
slowly
we dissolve

A Photograph

This poem is a photograph
to save her
in her floor-length dress asleep
on the bed
with the kitten, Julep &
Brandy, the mother
on the floor.

Her dress is red
& the candle
        snuffed
in the kitchen
the pork-chop bones &
apple skins
on the greasy plates

the sauterne bottle
in the dim light from the dining room
casts a green
shadow
across the table
           outside the window limbs
& branches
sing
with the wind.

1978

The Gulls

She stands in the shadow
of the cliffs,
her eyes holding
the sea's last glow.
As I pass
she turns slowly,
dark hair sifting
the salt air. I reach out
as if to draw from her darkening mouth
the smile.
            But no,
her eyes close to the wind.
Only the gulls
lifting & falling
over the sand.
Only her whisper: *Yes*

I know you. I am
your widow.

1981

The Dowser

She went right and left at once
and we lost her.
Never mind the new mattress,
it was a foul weather move,
a play on our weakness.

Minutes have passed.
The dowser's eyes claim
telling signals have begun to arrive.
His rod curves toward Venus.

This is impossible, gripes Boris.
Next we'll be splitting photons.
She's gone back to the fuchsia and
there's nothing we can do.

The dowser nods and says
he hears her giggling.

1986

The Ermine Violin

She wore it the way
a symphony swims the sublime
yet barely gets wet.

The ermine violin was a phase
in the life of music.
She understood.

It was finite
and described by dolphins
as they lunged the beaches.

It denied decay
and beauty disfigured: the melody
we were promised for the end.

The Space That Has No Negative

Evanescent, she said. It's you,
lying on the couch, your naked limbs
illuminating the room. You are sleeping,
and with each slow breath arises the body
taking you away. Now, above me, what remembers
enters me and stays. We are together,
and what we have that touches
holds continuous and warm
in a basin.

Here all movement bends
toward center, and our delicious stasis
tugs out and spreads. This is the space that has
no negative, that owns all and earns
each moment our freedom. A sphere
recording our future
as it grows.

1987

The Fruit Vendor

A cardinal has just split
the backyard
with red.
Sunday afternoon
in August, and across the porch you
lift your eyes from the ivy
and say:

> "I'm getting a message
> from an apple
> buried
> in concrete!"

I plan to work this
into the poem I'm writing,
about the young man
whose guide dog ran away
the day he fell
in love with the voice
of a fruit vendor,
the slim widow whose green
eyes he'll never see.

Summer Kitten

New kitty
        not just
a summer
replacement
        companion for us
and Brandy
who's hiding atop
        the refrigerator
        scared of
the new critter we've brought
for her love &
        pleasure

Takes time these
things
take time
        Julep's dead &
I wonder
if someone put
        in my lover's place
a stranger

How long would it take
would we ever
        meet on
steady footing
        reach
for each other

Brandy may
          reject the new animal
fear turned
hatred
          never softening

Does she remember Julep?

1991

Like Quartz

If I said I love her the way
I love rutilated quartz,
would she understand?

My love for lizards
and my love for her are not
the same, but what I feel

for nested fledglings, and
the brown and yellow salamander
with its wide grin, is mixed

with my love. The blue
wildflowers high in the dry
California hills remind me

that she is gentle, yet hardy.
Could she believe me if I claimed
my love is the lightning of

the aquatic garter snake
when it moves its single dorsal stripe
across a pond? I think of power

rising through her
from the earth to touch me,
and shriek with joy

like the Steller's Jay.

1995

A Crystal

To her who helps me bear
my personal cup

of trembling,
not that it pass

from me, but that I do not spill
nor dash to shards

the burden
I have been given.

The Kiss

Splash moonlight from the river
onto darkened stones.

When morning comes,
you'll see a broken yolk call the sun

to its yellow nest. Then raindrops, clear
as tiny thoughts of love, spread their bliss

over your face: your mouth
opens to a kiss.

Poem Kisses

She settles forward to take
his poem into her mouth.

Darting like a minnow, then pulling thickly back,
her tongue meets his syllables, repeats their shapes

the way the wings of a manta ray caress
the swelling sea. This touching

they do, this baring of sounds, is a long loving
of first kisses, strung and construed.

Shivering

Like a generous
grandmother

who wraps a stranger
in her woolen shawl,

you come to enclose
with your arms

my desperation. I am
filled, to shivering, with love.

A Wedding Toast

May your love be firm,
and may your dream of life together
be a river between two shores—
by day bathed in sunlight, and by night
illuminated from within. May the heron
carry news of you to the heavens, and the salmon bring
the sea's blue grace. May your twin thoughts
spiral upward like leafy vines,
like fiddle strings in the wind,
and be as noble as the Douglas fir.
May you never find yourselves back to back
without love pulling you around
into each other's arms.

2001

Life Path Rest Stops

The priest held open
the young man's
fly, airing out
his nest of notions
about love &
the Lord.

*

That I care for you
is unnatural, she said,
& God will make
me pay.

*

If you save the world
before you save
yourself, there'll be
no place in it
for you.

*

My body pities me,
she whispered, & pretends
to be drunk.

*

So bereft of beauty,
he found an
undermining ecstasy
in a mosquito
humming
near his ear.

*

Don't breathe—
this blossom has
its own star.

*

Between each breath
we learn to worship
the next.

*

Love is the only
answer
to death

2002

Arms

Sometimes she leaves
for the arms

of an idea, or
the idea

of another's arms,
but now, and

always, she
returns.

Asking

Please forgive
me if I keep

asking
your name.

Each moment
builds a new universe

and I need to find
you there.

The Gift

Their relationship moved forward
like a chrome bar

over the frets
of a guitar—each new stage

or resistance and release
brought music, as though

beyond their ken, some
ghostly hand was strumming.

Greed

He is indulging an honest
greed for real love.

His heart has an ambition known only
to maturity. When he touches,

he wants to reach the body within
her body, the body

that hasn't changed since before
she was born.

The Logic of Liquids

If we are vessels filled
with all that has been made one

by our love, and if loss is a siphon
drawing away from us what we hold dear,

splashing it back into the world—thus emptied
by grief, do we float higher, do we bob

lightly over this ocean of all
that love has broken?

Ogre

She is the scintillant ogre of the biomass,
and there are those whose nostrils widen to danger

when the breeze lifts. But with her a turtle
might find shelter, and perhaps a mouthful

of tasty gnats. When near, even a man
would fill with her loamy musk, would learn her

as she's learned the marshes
and the river.

Pocket Animal

I want to be there to wail
when your feral eyes

blaze. I'd be your pocket animal,
your packet of scat. I'd be fur for your sleep,

huddled close and trembling when wild
with dreams your claws might thrash.

And when it came time to move, I'd take
your scent away on my hooves.

Weather

There is a woman whose presence
encloses everything

like weather. He wants to be wet
in her rain. As he thinks this

the cock pheasant's call begins to sound
like sexual moans. His only desire

to do with her body
what air does to a feather.

2006

In Flowers: A Valentine for Anita

In morning sunlight, any bright patch of moss
will wink open with the green of your eyes.

Like the Virginia Rail, that leggy scooter
turning the lily pads up for lunch, you persist

in finding anywhere the images you need.
When I think of Goodwill bags, with their capacious

size, I remember your heart, beating deep for those
who struggle after life's smallest pleasures.

There's always a job to be done, and just like you,
your mud-speckled boots are ready. Marge Piercy says

we should favor those who have understood how to be of use,
and I treasure you, my busy friend. But sleep now,

my darling, my hand-held infinity, so I can write
my name in flowers across your dreams.

2009

The Blouses

Just the late afternoon light
dimly stroking

the park—no man of affection
would be satisfied with
so hesitant an approach. Then briefly

the clouds open their white blouses,
and the grass, the flowering
bushes say yes, yes, that's better,

that's what we've needed
all day!

Flares

Some part of me is in prison.
One of my gestures was, then wasn't,

then was a bullet. I feel like I've become
a card in the Tarot deck, but nothing

major. And there are rumors
going—I know them as a slight

irritation, the taste in my throat
that signals sickness.

Sun flares make the world strange.
Something is changing shape,

and I've heard it's my heart.

Her Breath

She is where the song
sits down and weeps

for joy, where the red-winged
blackbird calls for what comes

after. She is the river
splashing the moon onto darkened stones,

the broken yolk that beckons the sun
to its yellow nest. Her breathing

stitches what time
has torn.

Like Taut Persimmon

Come, lie down
where your hair may yearn
into the earth, where fear
is the last garment you fling.

Columbine and rain, azalea
and sunrise,
the world reaches
with two hands, two wings
over the hills.

Rest for a feathered moment
over the depths, then ease
your long-limbed spirit beyond
limitation. Stand naked
in the river of arrival.

Now wave to someone you love.

Like ripe pear, like taut
persimmon,
you fill
with mystical sugars.

Return to Manzanita

They took their failed love
to the Oregon coast, where

the early February storm
was monstrous and exquisite,
the beach covered four feet deep
with gelatinous foam, winds keening
at gale force and the rain horizontal
in volumes of wet. They kept

to the hill, inside their honeysuckle cottage,
where she built a fire that beckoned
wildly, and seductively, and softly until
it sank into its orange heart.

Then they moved closer, and gave
themselves to be consumed.

Split the Sun

She would split the sun
for him and
count twice
each scale of a salmon

at spawn. She would blow
milkweed pods
to pieces
just to show the breeze

where it's going. And when
the loon begins its
liquid moan,
the heat of her listening

would tip the grasses away
from the moon,
would shape
around them a nest.

That Sunday

I'm walking under willows, and when
she comes to me, it's with wrens.

Out hanging on the smallest branches I see wings
fluttering. Then feel, as I did once,

her hand like a feather on my neck.
"You've come back to me. You're home!"

But I am mistaken, and have been, and there
will be no wrens. I could have told her

how beautiful she looked with her hair free
and receiving the sunlight that day

in the park. But the sun
has gone.

To Make Mud

Can I say I want it all, want it now,
want it big and sweet
and twisty, want it small?
I want the scented fur
and good dirt beneath the nails.
Want to be there to wail

when her feral eyes blaze.
I want to touch with my tongue the lines
between her brows, to feel
where the tips of her soul
tingle.

I want the pledge of her, the fledge of her breast
and wings, the talons
of her protective heart. I want to make
mud with her, shape and flow
with her. I want the droplets

of dew festooned
along her cutting edge.
I want the tiny love-bomb
where she folds in.

I want to be her niche, her sack,
her sway-backed beast of love.

Touch the Blues

Say I'm a man of 53 years,
flexible in my thinking, yet shaped
by certain heavily reinforced concepts
about my relationship with the world.

Say I'm someone who cannot speak seriously
for long without blurting a phrase,
some winking word-curve that proclaims
I'm ready to ride pleasure
all the way to reverence.

Okay, I'm alone, stepping carefully down
metal stairs to a blues
club above a river in England. It's smoky,
and dark.
       Keeping my eye on the piano player,
because he's playing
brilliantly, and because the small stage
is a source of light,
I fumble blindly
for a table.
       I'm convinced if I look toward
the music I will find my way.
            Settled then into a chair,
I discover with pleasure I'm not alone here.
Her face glows with the blues.
          A shiver
ripples through my chest.
Despite a growing intimacy, I begin the usual
mental listing of setbacks
         until the sax lays down
a moan.

Shaking her head, my stranger
says, "It's okay. Don't."

She moves her hand, her naked
skin toward mine, and her voice gives birth
to the kind of phrase that changes
you: "Choose this chance to touch me."

Untamed

She has fully appeared,
yet he hears wings
and sees light fluttering
at the verge of shape, senses shadows
of yearning.

When she speaks,
his arms become flowering vines
that pull toward a mountain
rising.

An uneven,
untamed thing
could be set down between them,
and there it would be symmetrical, and
of beauty.

What Abides

As the years go, and you find
your view of the world

to be ever more identified
with history, it is a comfort

to have a field of study, a steady
involvement you return to each day—

something large and enclosing
which time does not transform.

In this way a love, or an abiding
friendship, might grow in value,

might become more true, as all
that promised you permanence

begins to twist and diminish
with the years.

What Water Says

Leafless aspens groom
the iced breeze, while below

a brook descends the mountain
with its musical story, remembering

the serenity of sky, and lightning's clear passion.
Water knows what is far will be near.

Water says choose that which closes distance,
choose touch. When snow falls

and a green mystery is carried
by all that moves,

choose love.

Wisdom

"I wake up like a stray dog
  belonging to no one."
                    —Jack Gilbert

Some days I don't want wisdom,
don't want art, just need to have someone near
to hear my silences, my large and little

noise. Never asked to be alone.
I'd take something as shallow as affection,
someone to ask me anything. Someone

to love me a chance to answer. I mean give me
as chance to give. A poet I was
wrote that when a love dies you carry

a heavy rock until you can't
anymore, and then mark where
you set it down. This is called

"Carrying the Stone." What a poet does
is carry his mark. I've said we draw nectar
from the fractures but I know

that's a lie. All love is one love
is another. I don't want all love,
I want hers. But I'd take anything

as deep as her hands dipped in my shallows.
If someone touches you are not alone.
Take wisdom. I need someone near.

2012

Bent Down

I'm alone, it's dark, I'm done
walking the beach
in the rain.

I was with no one
yesterday, and tomorrow
will be the same.

I enjoyed flirting with
the waves, letting them
almost catch me, wet me.

I know certain women who
have played that game.

But when I stopped and
bent down to lift free
of the sand a white

dollar shell, for that time
I gave myself fully. Wonder,
I do, why some good

person wouldn't come near
and give herself, wouldn't
want to.

Summer Pond

We each nibble toward the other
down a single stalk of grass
until we can wiggle our noses
and give each other a rabbit's kiss.

Our love well-fed, we hop off
hand-in-hand to gather moss
and warm leaves to fashion,
in the sun, a cozy bed.

There will be no sleeping
while chickadees pepper us
with questions and butterflies
perch where we are bare.

So we arise, bodies cloaked
in Summer breeze, and toe the path
to where a tepid pond
promises a sensuous bath.

NEW

Bus Station Blues

"I shouldn't even be here,"
she said. "I'd be creepy
if you knew me, and no one
would ever stay around."

She was chubby, had a puzzled
scowl, and there was something
in her hair that looked like
insect wings.

Didn't seem to be a danger.
Asked if she needed a ride.
She answered, "No." So I picked up
my bags and took her home.

Definitions of Love, No. 14

One nude Summer afternoon
your body will be a soft piano
with a million keys
being played by only the tips
of sunlight's fingers.

The Flirt

1.
Duck bobble.
Chemise.
So begins a love poem.

What I feel for language
is ardent, but not
simple.

Bowhead wail.
Peccary.
I blossom like the Great Purple Hairstreak

butterfly.
Bosom bodies.
I stroke the rippled syllables

and they stoke me hot.

2.
Don't need to raid
other languages
to find the charm.

But everyone knows English
is a flirt, so hey,
kiss me

in French and hug me hard
in Macedonian
Cyrillic.

Fill my soup bowl with chunky
Ogham Celtic,
and speed

me to bed in Native
Northwest
Lushootseed.

Fluency

The sound of the water over rocks,
repeating its mantra: we are this
fluency, fluency, fluency.

The sun steady over the towering trees
says nothing, but sees and knows all
this forest has ever done and, like my life

without you, my darling, there would be
no forest without the water and sun.

Folded

When in Oysterville
without the woman I love,
I feel deeply the damp chill
and seek the glow of foxglove.

I need to again be warm,
and measure how my heart beats
when I am folded in her arms
and find my loving retreat.

Four Legs and Six and More

1.
Were I a hedgehog, I'd be hungry,
always hungry for a fat insect.
Gimme two! Three I can handle.

I'm especially happy with critters
that crawl, that give a good crunch
when you bite down hard.

If a sliver of grass goes in with
the thick custard, then call it salad—
but don't say I graze!

2.
Where I come from, everybody burrows.
My uncles have left tunnels that generations
of six-legged travelers have used.

You want to throw a party
for family? Make sure you've got plenty
of hors d'oeuvres. Black beetles on the half-shell

are considered a delicacy. And to bring humor
to your celebration, you'll want to hire
a star-nosed mole to do impersonations!

Plan to finish the evening with fermented
bot-fly larvae.

3.
We bot-flies like to dig-in and burrow.
Then we pitch a tent just under
the skin: a dome-shaped station

that suits us fine. No tent-flaps, no real door.
When ready to leave, we go through
the red roof and do a little larval dance

in the late-summer breeze,
then drop greenward
for adventure.

How Deep?

How deep can you reach
before your fingers get cold?
Call it *dolors and scents*:
when people are sad, what
do they smell? And who will pay
for the fix?

Come near, little one—I have
a cushion here.
And for your nose
I offer a pink rose:
and too my whiskered cheek,
but be wary the thorns.

Mossforest

Exploring Orcas Island, near Obstruction Pass,
we found a metal post, hip-high

and seven or eight inches wide: it provided
a platform for a discrete and

complete rainforest of moss.
Valleys of dampness, ridges and rounded peaks

where the flora was most highly
individuated, with an aura where the dark

and willowy sexual organs towered
over a landscape that seemed to throb

with green. I wanted to be small enough
to live there with the woman

I love: in that perfect
region.

Not One

You are a flower too beautiful
to pick, too fragrant
to leave alone.

Like the hummingbird's
shifting bib,
you can be brilliant orange and pink,
or an earthy brown.

Even the dazzling green
of your eyes has moments of amber.

So when asked, my love, I must
confess you are not one thing,
and, like a faceted gem,

are worth turning
to catch the sun.

On a Photograph of an Orangutan Mother Holding Her Child

They are family, our family,
though it is with some wistfulness,
some shame, that one suggests kinship: her face
shaped by loving intelligence; the child's eyes
round owls of discovery and awe.

Yet there is hard experience
in the mother's forehead, and in the sad pockets
below her eyes. In all ways, from the earthy
color of their hair, to the delicate pink
of the child's ear, these are beings whose existence
incarnates the concept of Buddhist

Ahimsa: *We do no harm.*

We come in love, in love we leave.
When we are gone, for a brief time after
darkness falls on our species, the earth
may glow with
our absence.

Our Orcas Hours

The woman I love reaches
with her lens the fog
that like silken cloth slips over
the dark islands
and the angled rocky shore.

The woman who turns
and holds me while I sleep
also holds the sea, which is ever
shifting, ever becoming new.

Thousands of towering trees
imply their deep mastery of this land
of spotted deer, which bring their quiet,
and otters that curve into
and below the surf.

I would give this island a new name
to serve as a shining thread
to join all small and large lives with what lifts
us toward the sun unpeeling the gray clouds:
that name would be *Ahhhhh...*

Ravine

Were my mind a ravine,
there would be a creek
testing itself against the boulders
and fallen limbs.
Were my eyes amber jewels,
they would gather moonlight
to help scholars of the dark
do their challenging work.
And imagine my mouth
being a purse, which would
gather rather than spew.
My heart, then, would be
a clenched fist whose fingers
would loosen, its palm warm
to the touch of you.

Ravioli

When I was a young bachelor
living alone in a tiny apartment,
I fondly recalled the Italian dishes my mother
would cook for my father, and his seven kids.
So what did I do? Take my turn at cooking?
No. I wasn't that kind of bachelor. Instead,
I loved my cans of Franco American
spaghetti and Italian ravioli by Chef
Boyardee. A glass or two of red
jug-wine was often an added,
and welcomed, feature.

Refueling

Warned off by an empty
orange rubber glove
waving from the high limb
of a beach log, near where fallen
timber has blocked my path,
I turn around, leaving my footprints
in the sand as a series of S-curves
that create a wave form between
the water and high beach grass.
Then I'm back at the area identified
as a "Refueling Station for Shorebirds,"
where I find a comfortable seat.

This gray day is almost bright,
and the easy breeze across my face
reminds me of my own mother's
loving fingers. The sound of this large
bay, with a mountainous profile
in the distance, is soothing, and softer
than the clamor of ocean waves
two miles west over the peninsula.
Some days life seems so pleasant,
but where, I wonder, are those
famished shorebirds?

Said the Dragonfly to the Poet

We don't mind the beetles.
The mosquitoes are fakes.
The correct balance between sunlight
and moisture equals food.

As you know, we have wings,
and when the breeze has throttled
down, we are the undisputed
champions of the air.

When you've noticed we've settled
on a tall stalk of grass,
or fuzzy cattail, it's hands-off!
You don't pet a dragonfly.
And don't be shouting, or we'll
sew your mouth shut.

Also, it would please us
if you didn't laugh when you see
two of us conjoined while aloft.

When we're in the mood for love,
you can just move along—get back
to your wood and glass traps.
This delicious world
was not made for you.

Salmon Breathing

The Skagit Valley breathes
salmon: the in-breath

when salmon swim up
the Skagit rivers to spawn.

Then the streams cough
as dying salmon clog the shallows.

I love the easing out-breath
as hatchlings swim to the sea.

This cycle of the valley breathing salmon
has continued for thousands

of seasons, but has become irregular
and weak. I fear soon

there will be no salmon
bringing breath to the valley.

Shabby Love

My soul has been hacked,
and people I hardly know, or haven't
seen in years, have been asked
to send me love.

I know the appeal is fake,
but nonetheless wouldn't it be sweet
to be sent a little love by an old
friend, or literary colleague?

Sure, I wouldn't actually receive it—
the hackers would. And they
don't even spell my name correctly!
But how much could such a gesture cost?

Instead all I get are complaints
from folks who think it obvious
that my soul has been hacked. Complaints
are a shabby way to express love.

The Shallow End

Her postcard said, "The Grand
Canyon is no longer filled
with our love notes."

How can the only woman who
ever loved me for my viscera
be gone? She brought a warmth,

a dryness to my basement place.
People laugh when I say her moaning
incited riots in the roaches, but there's more.

I still have the half-empty bottle of clear
mucilage we used to adhere my contact lens
to her forehead—over her third eye. It clarified

her night visions, especially visions
of me. She always found my face; sometimes
organs too. How can I go on without her?

My spirit is a spreading stain. My mind
is drowning in the shallow end. Oh Loo.
Oh Loo-ga-roo.

Structure of the Universe

Richard Grossinger says, "the structure
of the universe
                  is the thought pattern
of the people."
                  Perhaps a bit
human chauvinist,
                  but sounds like
the Jesuit Teilhard
de Chardin
or some quantum mechanical
theologian.
                  What else
follows
the pattern?
                  Seems obvious:
the shape of a poem
                  the structure
of its thought.
Run it by faster, rethink it
at different speed?

Does our anxiety shift the cosmos?

Given Chaos Theory, which
suggests a butterfly's
                  wings
can cause a hurricane
thousands of miles and days
in the distance,
                  what effect will my sudden
mood-shift instigate
                  in the far reaches
of the Milky Way?

But the question most important
to me: is the body shaped
by its thoughts?
                    Can feeling
be spherical, love be two
spheres
            touching at all points,
one skin gloving
                    the other
to be one?

Is the universe modeled
on the empathy
of love?

A Sweetness

I'm remembering how fit, how strong
my father was well into his seventies.
He found no task daunting, and always
knew ways to build and repair things.

Yes, he was sometimes grumpy,
but I recall the last time we sat
outside in lawn chairs below the enormous
oak: our conversation ranged widely,

and there was in him a sweetness
I'd rarely seen. One thing that saddens
is that I never pressed him
to speak Italian, which might have

brought blossoms to the Old World power
and persistence he gained from
his Italian parents.

Thirsty?

If you feel thirsty, get down
and lick from the pond.

If hungry, tear the bark off
a sapling and begin to chew.

Tired of walking? Go float in the river,
but watch for what will drag you under.

Grown weary of your life? Stop groaning
and climb onto a cliffside with a view.

Think about flying. Imagine finding
the love you need. Now go home.

Valentine's Day, 2012: A Request
for Anita

You are my burning bush,
you bring color to my life,
and some days are my source
of heat! So yes, my life
is far more rich with you,
more complete. But one thing
I must ask: will you
marry me?

ACKNOWLEDGMENTS

A majority of the poems in this volume first appeared in the following literary journals and magazines:

Abraxas, Apple, Choice, Bellingham Review, Beloit Poetry Journal, Between the Lines, Cottonwood Review, Crab Creek Review, Dragonfly, Epoch, Five Willows Literary Review, Florida Quarterly, Foxfire, Gargoyle, Hearse, Indiana Review, Lillabulero, Manhattan Review, Minnesota Review, Nebraska Review, New Jersey Poetry Journal, New Mexico Quarterly, North Dakota Quarterly, Northwest Review, Notre Dame Review, Ohio Journal, Painted Bride Quarterly, Paris Review, Partisan Review, Ploughshares, Poet Lore, Poetry, Prime Time, Red Cedar Review, Road Apple Review, Rosebud, Seattle Review, Stinktree, Toucan, Trace, West Coast Review, Wisconsin Review and *Yardbird.*

James Bertolino's poetry has also been reprinted in over 35 anthologies.

The poem "A Droplet" which opens this volume was composed March 8, 1989.

Some poems in this volume have been selected from the following books:

Stone-Marrow, 1969, Anachoreta Press.
Becoming Human, 1970, Road Runner Press.
Employed, 1972, Ithaca House / Cornell University.
Edging Through, 1972, Stone-Marrow Press.
Soft Rock, 1973, Charas Press.
Making Space For Our Living, 1975, Copper Canyon Press.
The Gestures, 1975, Bonewhistle Press / Brown University.
New & Selected Poems, 1978, Carnegie Mellon University Press.

First Credo, 1986, Quarterly Review of Literature
   Poetry Series.
Snail River, 1995, Quarterly Review of Literature
   Poetry Series.
Pocket Animals, 2002, Egress Studio Press.
Finding Water, Holding Stone, 2009, Cherry Grove
   Collections.
Every Wound Has A Rhythm, 2012, World Enough
   Writers.

ABOUT JAMES BERTOLINO

James Bertolino's poetry has received recognition through a Book-of-the-Month Club Poetry Fellowship, the Discovery Award, a National Endowment for the Arts fellowship, two Quarterly Review of Literature book publication awards, the Connecticut College Contemporary American Poetry Archive and, in 2007, the Jeanne Lohmann Poetry Prize for Washington State Poets. His 27 poetry collections have been published by 21 presses in nine states, and *Ravenous Bliss: New and Selected Love Poems* is his twelfth full volume.

He has taught creative writing at Cornell University, University of Cincinnati, Washington State University, Western Washington University, the North Cascades Institute and, in 2006, retired from a position as Writer-in-Residence at Willamette University in Oregon. 2013 is the fifth year he has served as a poetry judge for the American Book Awards, sponsored by the Before Columbus Foundation in Berkeley.

He grew up in Wisconsin, and now lives on five rural acres near Bellingham, Washington with his multi-talented wife Anita K. Boyle, one horse, a dog and two cats.

Made in the USA
Lexington, KY
04 February 2017